Touching Souls and changing faces

www.samwellworldwide.com

Touching Souls and changing faces

A book by

SAMWELL

Touching Souls & Changing Faces

Published by Samwell Worldwide Ltd
www.samwellworldwide.com

ISBN: 978-1-9193333-0-4

Graphic design by 3RINGS
Cover and interior design by 3RINGS

First Edition
Printed in the United Kingdom

"Make impact beautiful." - Samwell

We
Us
Age
Race
Gender
People
All
Religion
Upbringing
Groups
Everyone
Humanity
Humanity
Connection
Interaction
Communication
Energy

Prologue Where he Found me.

This isn't a book about finding God.
This was my journey to spotting the divine in the mundane, an effort to point out the beauty that hides between breaths.

When I wrote it, this book was meant to be what I left behind, a final note to the world because I no longer wanted to live. The reason I say I didn't find Him is because, once I finished writing it, once it became my reason to stay, there He found me. Open arms. Warm embrace. No questions asked.

So worry not. These pages aren't laced with scripture, and they aren't here to preach.
They are here to remind you that someone is listening.
Someone hears you.
You are not alone.

I could have sat for years rewriting these pages as life kept teaching me new lessons, but it felt right to leave them as they are human, raw, and imperfect. Because that is exactly where they came from.

Contents

A Journey of Your Own

This book is an invitation, a space for reflection, growth, and connection. No matter your age, your background, or the experiences that have shaped you, this journey is yours to explore. The words on these pages are not here to tell you who you are or what you should become. Instead, they aim to offer tools, insights, and questions to help you reflect, grow, and connect in your own way.

Each chapter invites you to pause, consider, and engage with ideas that might resonate or challenge you. You may find some moments that speak directly to you, while others spark a curiosity to look deeper. That is part of the beauty of this journey; it unfolds differently for everyone.

This book aims to reach a variety of readers: from the young dreamer just beginning to navigate the world, to the seasoned soul seeking new perspectives. Whether it meets you fully or offers a single moment of reflection, the way you choose to engage is entirely yours.

Take your time. Engage with the ideas that call to you. And remember this is your journey, and no two paths through these pages will be the same. There is no right or wrong way to explore, only the one that feels true to you.

The first two chapters lay the foundation for what follows, introducing key concepts that shape the book. They may feel weightier, but they are intended to ground you for the journey ahead. Let them settle, and when you're ready, move forward at your own pace.

Welcome to this shared exploration. May it inspire you to see yourself, others, and the world in new and meaningful ways.

With love, from

SAMWELL

Meet Samwell

Welcome to Touching Souls and Changing Faces

Although I am a young man who spent my formative years dreaming of the stage, and now spend my days cobbling shoes and cutting keys in a small seaside town; I am no stranger to the human experience. I know what it means to miscommunicate, to hurt and be hurt, and I know I am not alone in this.

We live in a time where true connection feels out of reach, where compassion and understanding are in short supply. Voiceless heroes, silent strugglers, and those hiding behind the strongest façades often rise to the top, leaving empathy lost in the noise.

Do you ever feel like within yourself is not an adequate place to seek help?

Because I've felt this way at times, however this too shall pass, this feeling need only be temporary.

After surviving my years with my mind and having every label in the book thrown at me as a young adult, anything from chronic depression to ADHD and Aspergic tendencies, but after living with this for all time I have seen there is a solution within us all, and within this book I will break them down into four simple sections for you to carry with you into every new day stronger than the ones of the past and present.

Each section consisting of two chapters and a small reference chapter for understanding.

Let me start with the way in my own words I would describe life from the circumstances situations and traumas I have experienced,

"Life is a long and winding process of trials and tribulations that are destined to both aid and crumble us, it is essentially the pieces we choose to rebuild ourselves with that make us who we are today." - SW

With this in mind I will spare you the nitty gritty details of my past experiences and just say that they themselves have given me hope, they have taught me these tools, they have taught me to be compassionate and aiding to trauma in others, understanding to personal experiences and empathetic to attempts of communication and that an internal understanding is the simplest way of learning to authentically articulate and be heard.

I feel on a societal level these tools I have been taught are the ones we often leave behind, and they leave us unable to hear/be heard and to listen/communicate, these are the tools we will be putting at the forefront of our mind for a brighter future for all we come into contact with, including ourselves.

At this point I feel we all need to understand what we as humans were put here to do and if I were to put my opinion simply it would be, to touch souls and change faces, for the betterment of all.

Every person you have ever come into contact with has been at least marginally impacted by the way you treated them, as it has been said:

"They may forget what you said, but they will never forget how you made them feel." - Carl W. Beuhner

This is because emotional response is something we do not often control. I'm sure if you think back to school days, there are people who still make your heart flutter and those who still make your blood boil, these are all rational emotional responses of circumstance. Observed emotional response is what I would describe as our 'Conscious Witness' (Sense of I)

When we are not communicating with ourselves and removing our sense of ego (everything, what makes you a product of circumstance) that emotional response becomes the ruler of our lives.

With my understanding of these tools and the knowledge you are about to gain, both you and I will have the ability to use them to our advantage in everyday life. I personally have rapidly seen the positive impact that they have on both myself, others around me and the health, wealth and strength of the relationships I form both through work and in intimacy.

There is no more time for creating unhealthy habits and coping mechanisms, now is the time to flip the script on yourself. Don't wait for others to write your story for you, because they will.

Within the first chapters alone "Communicating with another sense of Self (I)" we will be assessing one of the single most beneficial tools from this book you and I will take into our daily lives and find that sense of comfort compassion understanding and communication where before we could not see it.

Once you have a feeling of understanding it puts you and every other sense of I on a level playing field regardless of authority. Because genuine human compassion and communication is the key to progress for both parties. These are the topics we will be discussing in this book, and these are the tools that shall allow you to touch souls and change faces the way we are intended to for ourselves and others.

How to Understand,

How to Question,

How to articulate,

How to empathise,

How to Communicate,

How to *Touch Souls and Change Faces*.

The Internal Observation

Communicating with another sense of self (I)

"Let's begin by exploring what I mean by our sense of I. Simply put, it's the 'I' at the start of every statement the one you use when you say, 'I am Samuel Witty.' You might think that 'I' is Samuel Witty, but the name is only a product of your environment and circumstance, I'm referring to the I that exists should we take away your name, your past, your trauma, that sense of simply 'I Am.' I will be referring to this as 'sense of I *(director)*.' the one who can aid through being and observe at ease.

In its rawest form, to me the term "Self" is the passenger that develops, grows and constantly adapts within a body made up of pure atoms. To me the "Self" is not Sam Witty the human, but the consciousness within my body. The term "self" many people I know refer to as what they are that can be seen and perceived by others. I will refer to this as 'sense of self *(Character)*.'

As said by Heraclitus.

"No man ever steps in the same river twice, for it is not the same river and he is not the same man."

This to me says about how our environments are ever changing and so are we as people, so the self *(Character)* is not something you are and remain, it is something that is constantly adapting and evolving towards situations and life.

This is the part of you that has ambitions, it has dreams, and my favourite the observer of your emotions. Have you ever been in a situation where you have been angry or sad or crying and that part of you thinks 'Are you done yet?'. That is the I in which I am talking about, the observer of Self. When I refer to 'Self' I simply mean that sense of I including all that your life entails, everything from traumas to habits to coping mechanisms.

I would advise looking at these as your 'director self' and your 'character self'. These can be two ways of looking at yourself in situations, you have a variety of tools as either of these in any given situation. A key thing to remember is that if you are using your tools you are having an impact, use your tools not only correctly but wisely.

This sense of I (Director) is within every sense of self (character) we communicate with.

This sense of I *(director)* isn't always aware that the sense of self *(character)* is simply a product of environment and circumstance, people are not always aware of why and how they act. Therefore, a beneficial tool for everybody Is therapy, A safe space where your sense of I can learn to understand why the self *(character)* acts and reacts the way that it does, and then creating tools and mechanisms to have them be the most productive. At the very least be your own therapist, learn to therapize, use your 'therapeyes'.

Now observing this from the sense of I *(director)* will not always be easy and there are many ways of doing this some people may opt for meditation or prayer, other ways include taking reflection time, breathwork, journaling, these are all powerful tools, however me and my ADHD mind found that the best way to do this is self-communication. Which in turn leads to an understanding that will allow for a very powerful thing, Self-compassion.

This is a deep understanding and knowledge of why you may act or react and that understand allows you to be your own guide through the process. Start by taking an example of a heightened negative emotion. (This exercise is also beneficial to do with positive emotions.)

Start by attempting to identify where you could classify this emotion, such as anger at a lady in the shop, ok where did this originate? Let's say frustration that she was taking too long escalated into an argument between the two of you. Were this the case does this stem from the fact she was inconsiderate of the way her taking her jolly old time affected those around her including you.

Ok so now we have identified todays heightened emotion of anger came from someone else's lack of compassion and consideration for others.

The two of you had an argument because you chose to speak up about the way it was affecting you and others. Now let's imagine you were not running late, and you still had this argument it would just be that you saw the affect it had on those around you, so your sense of self spoke up?

The fact your sense of self *(character)* and emotions got angry because you were also in a hurry could be because you are triggered because of someone else's lack of compassion to your situation. This is a perfect example of emotional response, and after an internal conversation you can understand that anothers lack of compassion for others affects you, this could stem from not being heard as a child, or not being valued by your peers and many other things but this is an example of the way you can take an inward conversation to progress.

Now next time in the store and the gentleman a few customers ahead is taking his time you feel a sense of anger and frustration from the lack of consideration however your sense of I understands that is a trigger for your sense of self and should not feel like a personal attack that should provoke an emotional response. I would advise you do this as often as possible, have these internal observatory conversations see what provoked the self's emotional response from the perspective of the observer, from the I's Eyes.

I suggest taking a moment now.

You can begin with the following statement,

"I am here to see how my sense of self has been affected today, let us reflect."

So now let us take into consideration the way another person's emotional response can affect you and does affect you.

If we use our sense of I *(director)* to observe our emotional response, the response itself becomes secondary and an understanding can be at the forefront.

Another example of this internal conversation may be, "I am feeling very anxious now within this conversation, ah it could be because this figure is very a powerful and I feel a lack of self-worth and a lack of compassion from the person I am speaking with."

This internal conversation can then be taken further with this sense of I *(Director)*. We as human beings are very compassionate, empathetic and good at reading each other you can ask yourself "so where does this powerful figure stand and what gives them the power to affect my emotions?" Not to say the case will always be the same and you will always be right but for your sense of self *(Character)* the conversation with the I *(Director)* can be very beneficial. "Does the way this powerful person communicates with me give me the feeling they were never heard so they push their ideas and presence onto others? Could they have been belittled as a child? Could it be from a lack of authority?"

You will find once these questions start flowing you start to seem to understand more the sense of I *(Director)* you are communicating with, you start to see the I *(Director)* within them and how perhaps trauma or circumstance has affected the way the choose to communicate and portray themselves, and as if by magic the sense of I within you both will begin to communicate.

This does not mean it is best to ask the person these questions especially in a business environment it is simply to give you a chance to communicate on a more pleasant plane for yourself. People may still not allow you to feel heard and that is ok because with a sense of understanding of all the circumstances and environments leading to this conversation might make that difficult for them. We will be divulging further into the ways of understanding, relating to communicating with others with a removal of your sense of self *(Character)* in the next chapter, for now we will be looking further into how to communicate and understand your own sense of self *(Character)*.

If we take a moment to look at the pandemic as an example people as a whole had time to observe themselves, to sit in reflection and a chance to wake up to the traumas of their past and this has created both healthy and negative thinking patterns.

Our sense of I *(Director)* has had time to work out what is going on to why our Self *(Character)* feels inadequate or undervalued or maybe powerful and productive, but it indeed has given us time for the internal conversations to work out where we stand and the positions, we and others put ourselves in.

The voice in our head we use for these conversations is our

most beneficial tool but also incredibly smart at picking us apart after all it knows everything about us it is the observer of not only emotion but progress, behaviour, habits and everything else our sense of self entails. It knows the dreams you haven't committed to and the ideas you gave up on, but when it pulls us apart this is conflict not from the I *(Director)* but from the sense of self *(Character)* battling with the I.

It is your job as the I *(Director)* to keep the self *(Character)* and emotions in check, now these emotions are not necessarily always a bad thing they want progress and despise being stagnant, A wise man once said to me "Sam don't settle dust settles." And my I often reminds my sense of self *(Character)* this and that is when the self picks apart my shortcomings whereas the I *(Director)* was simply trying to inspire progress.

I also often tell myself, dust does settle and it is progress towards needing cleaning, everything is progress towards something.

There may be things that were never an issue for you before that are now being pulled apart like an old sweater this is simply conflict between your I *(Director)* and your sense of self *(Character)*, allow them to communicate and work out the best solution for progress, don't just settle for an imbalanced internal conversation, learn how to communicate within yourself for the product of self-compassion to lead to a brighter future for yourself and all those you meet along your journey.

Without having a sense of self, there will come no self-respect, leading to a lack of reciprocated respect for and from others with no regards for the possible outcomes and effects of each other's actions.

Another issue is no self-recognition, meaning you may not see your potential and therefore not achieve your ultimate capabilities, leaving people in their final moments wondering what more they COULD have done for their own personal benefit and growth.

The Mirror and the Window

Observation begins within a mirror reflecting the depths of our thoughts, feelings, and experiences. This mirror shows us who we are, what we carry, and how we perceive the world. But the mirror alone is not enough. To truly understand, we must also step toward the window, looking outward to see how the world reflects back at us.

The mirror and the window are in constant conversation. What we see within shapes how we interpret the outside world, and what we observe outside informs the stories we tell about ourselves. It is in this exchange that we begin to uncover the intricate link between self-awareness and understanding others.

As you move forward, take a moment to reflect:

What do you see when you look into your internal mirror?

Are there patterns, assumptions, or fears that shape the way you see the world?

How does your understanding of yourself influence the way you interpret others?

Take these questions with you as a guide for the next chapter. Explore the ways in which your inner world affects your perception of the outer world and vice versa. Let this be a moment to pause, reflect, and begin the journey toward deeper insight.

The External Observation

The attention to the senses of self (I) around you

Now let's look back at the lady you argued with in the shop as our situation to observe, let's take into account the sense of I within all of the characters around you. To set the scene there is the person behind the till, the lady in front of you and a line of 3 customers behind you.

Take a look at the one behind the till, how are they feeling? We can observe this easily; we don't have to start contemplating their past traumas and upbringing. Let's say she also looks frustrated by the lady taking her sweet time (Observation Number 1). Now we will look at the queue behind us, is anyone particularly frustrated? In a hurry, itching to get somewhere? (Observation Number 2). The lady that is taking her sweet time, does she appear to be struggling with something? Or frustrated herself that she is holding everybody up? (Observation Number 3). Then finally within ourselves is this getting us angry? Do we

need to hurry the situation along for ourselves? Is this overwhelmingly inconvenient for us? (Observation Number 4)

Observation number One.

How is this person feeling and are they being dramatically impacted by the situation? If no let us move on, If yes, the solutions will all become clear the more we divulge into further sections of the book.

Observation Number Two.

How are the senses of self around you feeling and reacting to the situation you are all being placed in? Can you sense that one of the three are extremely anxious and need some sort of aid? Is someone about to blow their top and you can see the tension building within them? Does someone have any form of characteristics to show they may suffer with a mental disability, and you can tell how uncomfortable they are feeling?

Observation Number Three.

How is this person the influencer of this frustration being affected? Is it also negatively affecting her? Is she struggling and may be in need of assistance or simply oblivious to the frustration she may be causing?

Observation number Four.

Not to say you should always leave yourself till last, however in most scenarios once you have analysed the emotional state and reactions of those around you, you simply put yourself in a better understanding of how you may be feeling. Take a look within and if you've got the time (Which in this case you do) give yourself a moment for the reflective exercise. "I am here to see how my sense of self is being affected right now, let us explore." See where this internal conversation takes you.

Now after taking some time to explore the emotional state of those around you and the sense of Self within you; Once we do a little more exploration into how to properly read and analyse the senses of self around us we will be moving on to learning how to act or react in more than just our "pop to the shop" example.

We will be looking into three main questions within the remainder of this section, all accompanied with exercises or examples to help guide you along your understanding.

The three questions we are going to explore in *Chapter 2i* are as follows.

- **Where does your sense of self see similarity or understanding within the other sense of self?**

- What does the removal of your sense of self and observing as the I (Observer) do for the situation?

- Where does emotion rule over the I (Observer) in the sense of self you are observing?

The Questions of Chapter Two

Where does your sense of self see similarity or understanding within the other sense of self?

Where does your sense of self (not I) see things within another sense of self that relate directly to it? This could be seeing that someone has a trait of talking over people and you know you do the same. Take a moment to observe why you do this, it could be something as simple as feeling like you were not heard as a child and were told you were wrong when you knew you were right. Which led you to as an adult blurting out your opinion if you feel strongly about something or know yourself to be correct.

Perhaps you notice that a person you are with is irrationally tapping their foot or jigging their knee in the café/restaurant, and you think back to the way exams used to make you nervous so your legs used to bounce under the table, perhaps this sense of self is feeling a presence of anxiety that you may not be able to relate to, but you understand where its manifestation may stem from.

There could be a case of a woman at your work is incredibly uncomfortable and always leaves early when the manager on shift is male. Within yourself you may have experienced a time where a person of the opposite sex who wears glasses made you extremely uncomfortable and for a while you found it hard to make eye contact with people with glasses.

You may not be able to relate to the potentially extreme circumstances leading to the colleagues extreme lack of comfortability, but you can understand how their sense of self and emotions is running away with the observer (I) and not letting them commit to their shift, even when the male in question isn't directly responsible.

When you start to relate your own traumas to the minor or extreme responses of others, you create a playing field for conversation through empathy and understanding. This could be your friend who has been suffering from depression for many years and you understand how they feel because of some dark places you went to after a traumatic experience. All of these are examples and do not mean directly compare yourself through conversation in effort to aid another person, these are examples of an internal dialogue to relate your sense of self to another's, to progress into meaningful communication.

What affect does the removal of your sense of self do for this situation?

Now for this I want you to take a moment within your observation of others and remove your sense of self. Yes. All that work we just did to relate in an effort to learn to empathise through experience, get rid of it, take it all away.

We are now going to simply look as our sense of I (The Observer) and take away what we may perceive through relational thought and instead only apply relative thought, as though you have no sense of self, no traumas, no habits, no comfortability. You are no longer a product of your environment; you are simply the I Am.

This is a beneficial tool when looking internally and should be done when we do our exercise of "I am here to see how my sense of self has been affected today, let us observe."

Now this is something we project outwards. Something we use to look into the way another person may be feeling, without our own personal connotations to a situation or circumstance. We are going to look at simply how this person is affected.

To do this we simply are going to try to understand what this persons sense of self could be a product of. We can observe the way they communicate with us and project onto us as we did before. Now think how this could have affected past relationships they may have had. We can look at how this may have been a product of goals unreached, heights they may have accomplished based on the information given to us in the past or just the current conversation. To do this we are simply attempting to listen to their sense of (I) in order to gain knowledge of their sense of self. How do they dictate they feel when they say, "I was mad about x, y or z."? What do these explicit referrals of I communicate about their sense of self?

This can often be confusing, but you will find with the more internal and external observations you make, the easier it becomes to understand a sense of self communicating their effect of their sense of I. So, when someone says. "I am disappointed with myself man; I was meant to get these things done today and I only did half." Observe that regardless of the work done by them their sense of self is pulling apart their sense of I (The observer) because they did not achieve a laid-out expectation. From there we can begin to question whether this is because of a heavy expectation placed on them by others, a desire to please people and took on more than they could handle, or a habitual nature of wanting to achieve more that they are capable of.

This could come from many places and removing your sense of self and simply observing as they communicate with you, you may start to put more together from the information given. The way they regard friends and family, the way they perceive failure, and you can come to some not always accurate but progressive solutions in order to aid them with their process. Anything from scheduling advise from your sense of self to observatory ideas from your sense of I.

Is emotion in control of this persons observer? Where does it sit?

For this you will need to be able to use both your sense of self and your observer (I). You will investigate the persons genuine emotional responses how their achievements, failures, traumas, and experiences make them feel upon projection. (Top tip it's not always beneficial to point these out especially to strangers, but in understanding they aid the communication process.)

So, when they discuss with you their failure to complete a set number of tasks, what does their emotional response entail, how does it affect their gaze, their posture, their tone of voice. How does it change the way they communicate with or view themselves?

There are plenty of things to be aware of and to pay attention too, does their demeanour remind you of that of someone struggling with anxiety or depression? Someone who lacks self-esteem? Someone who is too proud to show their pain, or someone who does not want to burden you with their issues? Observe this. Really consider whether they decide to be combative with your attempt at aid to make you aware they do not want help, or do not want to feel like they need it. Or whether their defensiveness comes from a place of having to portray strength for those around them.

We also need to consider the fact that some of these emotional responses may be habitual, they could have been created as coping mechanisms from past trauma, and while it may not be our job to pick that apart and 'fix' in order to touch souls and change faces the way we were meant to, we need to be able to understand how. To communicate with and aid them for the better.

There are a whole variety of things that need to be taken into consideration from mental 'disorders' to coping mechanisms of trauma. But this does not mean you have to walk on eggshells, it means you need to be able to communicate with the sense of I within us all, because that brings a sense of comfortability. If you are like me, you know that we seek communication. Genuine authentic and compassionate communication. To do that we need to be more observant of the way our words impact others, the way others words impact us, and the way we can use this information to aid those around us, even if their emotions are running away with their sense of I (The Observer).

Now that we have looked at both Internal and external observations, I would like to take a look at what I imagine to be the purest of examples and I call this the inquisitive nature of children.

Next time you are around a child I would like you to look for these characteristics, think of a child as an anxious but carefree mind one that has no connotations yet still has the desire to learn communication and understanding. A child will provoke a reaction and then observe the response this may be dropping something to see how It affects you the individual. How it provokes your actions compared to those whose reactions they are used to observing. This is done incredibly smoothly with the action quickly followed by an observation, an example of this was my niece. She looked at me to see if I was paying attention to her and then dropped a piece of her food onto the floor and then very quickly looked back to me to observe my reaction as the only other person in the room.

Another example of this is watching Television I observed

her watching, and then when something of impact happened that provoked thought within her she would sharply turn her head to me in an effort to determine how this had impacted me. When I laughed, she began to release the laugh she had been holding whilst observing me as she had seen it was the 'appropriate' response to this situation.

It was apparent that her attempts were not simply to observe then copy the responses of those around her, but to learn if her responses were correct (appropriate.)

This is where the idea of learned behaviour comes into question. What was projected onto our parents in most cases was projected onto us as children. Simply because we picked them up as appropriate responses. As we grow up it is our responsibility to determine what is appropriate for ourselves, instead of continuing the cycle of projection.

However, it seems to me that in a lot of instances this inquisitive nature, this observatory period comes to an end, when and why are the questions we should be asking ourselves.

Perhaps because we transition from enquiring to being told who and what we are, the accumulation of labels we are both given and self-prescribe, tie us to the self we know and believe to be ourselves.

While we have all heard the phrase don't judge a book by its cover, observing appearance can give characteristic clues. But should not be used as the entire backbone of our observations.

You will never fit the essence into anothers cover.

The Stories We Tell

Observing the world is more than just seeing, it is about understanding the stories that shape us. Each of us carries an internal narrative, a collection of experiences, beliefs, and reflections that inform how we see ourselves and the world. But these stories do not exist in isolation; they are in constant dialogue with the people and events around us.

When we truly see others, their struggles, their joys, their vulnerabilities, we open a doorway to understanding our own stories more deeply. Observing the lives of others can make us aware of the common threads we share and the unique patterns that define us. In seeing another's resilience, we might reflect on our own strength. In witnessing another's pain, we might find the courage to face our own.

Take a moment to reflect:

What stories do you carry about yourself?

How have these been shaped by your observations of others?

Think of someone whose story has inspired or challenged you.

How did their journey affect the way you see your own?

In what ways can understanding others' stories help you rewrite or expand your own narrative?

This next chapter steps into my story, a reflection of both my internal world and the way I have seen and been shaped by others. As you read, consider how your own observations might illuminate the story you are still writing.

The Book of Samwell

A product of multiple environments.

I am a product of multiple environments, as are we all, they have shaped who I am and taught me the lessons I share. These come from places of misunderstanding and a lack of compassion, from manipulative, belittling and mentally corrupting authority figures and many forms of abuse in the places I wished to consider safe.

I had to learn to communicate to people in a way that would avoid conflict and tension, I had to learn to be silent and observe for my own longevity, I had to learn to feel safe when I did not. I had to learn the be the silent analyst of those around me in an attempt to avoid conflict for those I loved or chose to spend my time with.

I had to learn to do what I could to achieve unrealistic standards and fulfil jobs that were not my burden to bear, I had to become this person and through dealing with this and its impact my whole life, I have learned exactly what not to do and what I find works to aid.

These circumstances have made me the man that I am today, the one who wishes to aid even those who wish him ill. The man who wishes to provide hope for those who also do not see it. To show the light within the world we live in and the environments we are placed in.

I have learned that through the tools I am sharing within this book, even from the darkest of places the light can be found.

My experience of homelessness was a deeply unsettling period of my life, though I know it may not look like what many imagine when they hear the word 'homeless.' I was not sleeping rough on the streets, but I had no stable place to call home. For a time, I was moving from one friend's sofa to another, eventually living in a caravan, paying cash in hand for short-term shelter. While I was fortunate to have temporary options and a network of support, I felt the constant weight of insecurity the sense of being unmoored, uncertain, and reliant on the kindness of others to get by. I recognize that my situation was not as dire as it is for many who face homelessness. I never had to sleep rough on the streets, and for that, I am incredibly grateful. But I also came to understand that homelessness is not a singular experience. It can look like sleeping in a car, staying in shelters, or, as in my case, moving from one temporary arrangement to another. Each version comes with its own challenges and emotional tolls.

My time without a stable home taught me a deep respect for the resilience of those who navigate this reality, whether for weeks, months, or years.

This time in my life taught me not only about the fragility of security but also about the profound importance of kindness, community, and understanding. It reshaped the way I think about stability and privilege, and it gave me a deeper empathy for the unseen struggles that so many face. It is a reminder that even when life feels unsteady, small gestures of support whether a sofa offered, or an ear lent can make all the difference.

This book exists because I reached a point in my life where I no longer wanted to be alive. I had decided that my time here was done, and in those moments, I began to write not for myself, but for those who felt as I did. This book was meant to be the legacy I would leave behind, something to show others who were struggling that they were not alone, that the weight they carried could be lightened, and that the despair they felt didn't have to be permanent.

As I wrote, something began to change. Through the process of putting these thoughts into words, I found hope. The birth of my son gave me a purpose beyond myself, a reason to stay and make an impact. It was through the writing of this book and the love I found for my son that I decided I would stay to show that life, even in its darkest moments, is worth living.

I wanted those debating the choice I thought I would make to know there is another way. Through impact, kindness, compassion, and empathy, life can be meaningful, even beautiful. I wrote this book for you, as a guide and a reminder that, even in the darkest times, there is light to be found. Life is worth living, not just for what we achieve, but for the impact we leave on others and the connections we create.

Seeing Through Change

Observation is not static; it evolves as we do. The way we see ourselves, others, and the world shifts with each new experience, revelation, and challenge. Life invites us to adapt not just in how we act, but in how we perceive. What once seemed unchangeable may begin to shift, and what once felt invisible can suddenly come into focus.

Our stories, as explored in the previous chapter, are not fixed. They are rewritten with every choice we make and every truth we uncover. Growth requires us to revisit our narratives and challenge the way we see the world. It asks:

What assumptions are you holding onto that no longer serve you?

What new perspectives have your experiences revealed?

Adapting our observations is not a sign of inconsistency; it is a testament to growth. To see through change is to honour how far you have come and to remain open to the lessons yet to come.

Take a moment to reflect:

Think of a time when your perspective on someone or something changed completely.

What caused the shift?

How has growth in your own life reshaped the way you observe others? Yourself?

What might happen if you allowed your current beliefs and perceptions to evolve even further?

The journey ahead asks us to embrace the evolving lens of observation, understanding that our changing perspectives are not weaknesses they are signs of life. As we move forward, let us carry both curiosity and humility, knowing that every shift in perspective brings us closer to seeing the truth of ourselves and the world around us.

The Adaptation of Observations

Seeing with your observer

We now understand our personal and external observations, or at the very least have an idea of where we are going to start on our journey. It is now time to divulge in the fact that our observations are adaptive. Over time as we continue to do these observations, not only will the idea of looking at others as the unique sense of self become more beautiful to witness, but we will also start to notice the Sense of I (The observer) of these persons emotions, we can see the way that the more light brought to that witness impacts them, and the way this moulds their view of themselves. We can see through communication that we are able to influence the self to notice the witness within all of us.

This is adaptive observation, the way that as time progresses, we can notice the changes in a persons actions and intentions based on the way they are viewed by themselves and others, and I do not doubt that with the skills you are learning, people will notice your attention to them.

It is unfortunately rather uncommon that people communicate with your sense of I, and observe your sense of self and take all of these things into consideration. But the way your relationships and observations will adapt will be for the better of those around and within you. Over time you will see your emotional vocabulary and range will indeed expand as you explore the extents the mind and self will go to influence the sense of I (The Observer). This in itself is incredibly adaptive, your conversations become more meaningful, your connections become more authentic and the resonance you share with others has a spark that people will notice.

As time goes on you will notice flaws in your own observations, you will see where things are wrong habitually and this could come down to the sense of self and the ideas you project. This could come from the removal of self and missing something you can relate to. Over the years I have been no stranger to misreading and interpreting the way another feels (especially when these emotions are ones projected TOWARDS my sense of self.)

But this is part of the beauty of observation and after my lifetime thus far doing this I've learned to accept where my reading of the situation is wrong because of my own mechanisms and triggers, and where they are wrong because of the projection of the other in the engagement. I'm not promising you that you will be able to read minds and get every interaction right.

But through observing, seeking similarity, removing self, and noticing where emotion rules response, you will be able to impact the lives of those around you for the better.

The Lens of Relation

Every observation exists in context shaped by who we are, where we stand, and the connections we hold. Our relationships, even fleeting ones, act as lenses that colour how we see the world and ourselves. The way we interpret someone else's experience whether it is joy, pain, or struggle is always influenced by our own internal world.

Even the most minimal of personal experiences can offer us a window into someone else's extreme experience. While our experiences may not compare directly, the insights we gain from our own nuanced feelings, grief, doubt, hope, or love, can help us understand the emotional echoes of another's story. This does not mean we can fully grasp their reality, but it does mean we can find threads of connection that foster empathy.

In relationships, we often see reflections of ourselves, but we also gain glimpses of what lies beyond our understanding. The lens of relation asks us not to compare, but to connect, to notice the ways we are both similar and different, and to honour the truth in both.

Take a moment to reflect:

Have you ever found yourself relating to someone whose life feels vastly different from your own?

What made that connection possible?

How might your understanding grow if you allow yourself to explore the emotional similarities, rather than focusing on the differences?

As we move into the next chapter, consider this:
How do your own experiences, even small ones, shape the way you see others?

Relative

Observations

Taking note with understanding

Now using the observative techniques we learned in external observation, such as similarities within our observation of self, and the observations of the self we will be communicating with. We will now be looking at what I describe as relative observation.

Where does the information gained put you in terms of making an impact?

When you notice and draw attention to someone's happiness that you can form a connection with, for example their new pet, you create a direct resonance that can have a beautiful positive impact on the person you are communicating with. The genuine resonance is felt by both parties and can have a knock-on effect for the rest of the persons day. The genuine resonance of a feeling of happiness can enlarge this feeling within you both.

This can also be seen when you have a direct resonance with someone's accomplishments on a major and minor scale. Someone who is depressed has a conversation with you about how today they actually got up on time made their bed and did the laundry, now to most people this would be 'ok great you did something that most people do.' However, if you can get to a place of understanding and resonate with this person, the positive impact it could have on their next day because of the love and reciprocation they received the day before, could be the motivating factor that they need for progress.

If we take the above example of someone with depression, if you are someone who has spent time in a depressed place and managed to overcome this, communicating this without trying to be a teacher. Simply communicating it through understanding and authentic empathy for where they are, using the information you have gained from personal experience can actually promote immense progress within someone who may not have seen progress as an option. This can change their outlook to progress being inevitable. Approaching a situation through relation in an effort to directly teach someone, can very quickly promote the idea of inadequacy within someone, especially if they are already fighting internal battles. This is why external observation is important, remember, you will not be able to observe everything. So even if you have not noticed this feeling of inadequacy, it still is not something you should ever wish to project onto someone.

Of course, we are discussing relative and relational observation, but this does not mean they have to be of an exact nature of the self you are communicating with. The similarities of emotion from different triggers and circumstances still lead to great tools of progression. The relation of emotion leads to a more understandable form of storytelling that has a better chance of your audience or conversational partner relating to it.

Where is this knowledge relevant?

If you are using the tools of internal and external observation to only discuss your own progress and or regression, this can become very manipulative in nature. These tools are for the betterment of self and those around you.

If you are persisting in conversations of regression of self or the person you are interacting with, this can create a very negative environment. While it is important to use adaptive observation to see how someone is changing over time; the use of this to point out their lack of progress alone will not have the intended impact of aiding people for the better. The use of these skills to note how someone is changing over time is a very important skill and opens up beneficial conversations. Not only can this help someone keep a track of their own progress and/or lack thereof. It also shows a genuine interest, and this is great for the sense of self and I within the one you communicate with. This can promote self-worth with someone seeing that another self has genuine investment and interest in their wellbeing, this can promote leveraged impact on those this person comes into contact with.

Taking the time to constructively note someone's regression is also beneficial and can have a positive impact, because again it shows authentic investment in this persons wellbeing.

The relative observation allows the other sense of self to appreciate the sense of self within you. It is important to note the persons ability to resonate with the communication you are trying to have in this moment. They may not have the emotional capacity or stability in order to talk about it; and this is something we need to be able to understand. I'm sure with some internal observation and reflection we can relate to a time of similar feelings, the aim is to then promote comfortability, not provoke an unpleasant conversation.

Another exercise of relative observation is looking at when you are an interactive party and when you are a background character for the people around you. This is an observation that is best done in the coffee shop experiment, or perhaps at a family function or party and observe to whom you are an interactive part of conversation and is being included in conversation, and to which senses of self within the environment that you are just in the background, and they do not observe your emotional and physical responses.

From Seeing to Impact

Observation is the seed; impact is the bloom. Noticing the world around us opens the door to influencing it, but impact requires action. It is the choice to take what we see and use it to create ripples, small or large that touch others in ways we may never fully grasp.

Impact can be instant, like a kind word that brightens someone's day, or lasting, like a decision that changes the course of a life. Both are powerful, and both begin with the act of truly seeing.

Unless willing to fall as an acorn again,
The mighty oak is destined for lumbar.

Your smallest impact today could ripple through the fabric of someone's existence forever, how would you want that to look?

Reflect for a moment:

When has a small action made a significant impact on you?

What ripples are you creating, whether intentionally or not?

How can you turn observation into meaningful action?

As you move into the next chapter, explore the nature of impact, its immediacy, its longevity, and the difference it makes on the lives we touch.

The Book of Impact

Leveraged and instant Impact

The way I look at impact is as a ripple of energy, this echoes through everything we do or the person we impact does. The idea that you reading this book means that any influence that you have taken into your life, will in turn have impact on every person you ever come into contact with. With the intention of Touching Souls and Changing Faces, we can all impact the world for the better through leveraged impact. It is our duty as a collective, to share love through compassion and understanding, and this does not mean others can simply do wrong and we understand, and their actions become irrelevant, it means that through our understanding we can teach others to understand their wrongs and have the impact they need for progression.

The people in and around our lives do incredible things and they often go unnoticed, and one of the most powerful things you can do is to give them their roses, (a gesture of recognition, the flowers for the work they have done.)

I myself try to hand praise out like it's candy and every day is Halloween

I'm sure you see the issue in this, it would be easy for these to be viewed as hollow but with the correct observation and intention they should bloom in the hands of those you provide them with. Most people work hard, most people do love, but it is the feedback received along the way that taints future progress, we need to show our appreciation of effort. Give out your roses every day, they will die held to ourselves. Give the same person roses everyday if you see fit, appreciation is a powerful influencer, and it shows people the genuine care you have for them. The roses kept to ourselves will not bloom, do not wait till someone is gone to give them the flowers they deserve.

I would now like to describe to you my analogy for we as people. Think of us as a collective as a tree.

The people, the we, the us, the everybody, we are the leaves different unique individuals all with their purpose to aid the tree.

The branches of the tree are how we have categorised ourselves, these are our 'dividing factors' anything from gender, to religion, to upbringing, to age, these are the groups we self-prescribe.

The trunk of our tree is humanity as a whole, the thing that connects us all, the fact that we are what we are, Human.

The roots are our communication with one another, they are our intentions, our energy and our sense of connection to the earth and the other senses of self.

So, although we are all the same, the leaves providing sunlight to our collective, gaining energy through the roots and our connection, the only thing that breaks us up is our observation that those leaves are from a different branch. Does this not seem almost trivial?

It is also important to observe where your editing of prior commitments affects the other self that is involved in those arrangements.

Us
We
Age
Race
Gender
People
All
Religion
Upbringing
Groups
Humanity
Everyone
Humanity
Connection
Interaction
Communication
Energy

The Ripple's Return

Every impact we make sends ripples outward reaching others in ways we may not always see. But those ripples do not just vanish; they return to us in the form of emotional responses. These responses, whether immediate or delayed, reflect the ways our actions touch others and reveal deeper truths about our own intentions and desires.

Love and lust, desire, ambition, isolation, each response carries a story, a mirror of both the one who feels it and the one who inspired it. Love might be the echo of connection, while ambition could rise from the spark of admiration or envy. Isolation may reflect vulnerability, a need for space, or the shadow of misunderstood impact.

Let this be an invitation to observe not just the ripples you send, but the waves that come back.

The ripple's return asks us to listen, to truly hear, to genuinely observe.

Reflect for a moment:

What do the emotional responses of others reveal about the impact you have made?

How do their reactions influence the way you see yourself?

Are you open to learning from these echoes, or do you shy away from the reflections they offer?

As we step into the next chapter, we will explore these responses more deeply, how they may be born, how they are felt, and how they offer us a chance to understand the reach of our impact.

Reading

Responses

Understanding the self we communicate with

In this chapter we will break down some responses and try to give an understanding of what may influence them. From there it is an open ballpark. It is using your skills of observation and internal investigation to work out what they mean.

Remember everyone is an individual and the way they think and react is a product of circumstance. These responses will mean something different to everyone who picks up this book, so take a moment to analyse what they mean to you before diving into the breakdowns I am going to share. The emotional responses we are going to cover in this chapter are as follows:

Love & Lust
Ambition
Reclusion
Desire
Hostility

Love and lust

Love is more than just an emotion; it's a connection that flows through everything in life. It's what ties us to each other, what inspires growth, and what makes us feel truly alive. Lust is part of this same energy, an intense, immediate attraction that draws us into the present moment. Together, they reflect the ways we connect with others and with the world around us.

Love is the steady rhythm; the enduring bond that helps us grow. It teaches us to see ourselves in others and to care deeply not just for the people we love but for the world as a whole. It is what encourages us to be better, to expand our hearts and minds, and to find meaning in the connections we make. Lust, on the other hand, is the spark, the thrill of being drawn to someone in a way that is instinctive and electric. While love is about the big picture, lust reminds us of the power of the moment.

Both love and lust are part of the same energy, the same drive to connect and grow. Lust can lead to deeper love, just as love can reignite the spark of lust. When we understand these feelings as parts of a larger whole, we see that they are not just about relationships with others they are about understanding ourselves and the ways we are all connected.

Desire

Desire is a powerful force that shapes much of what we do. It is the feeling that pulls us toward people, things, or goals that we believe will make us happy or fulfilled. But desire is often built on how we perceive something, not necessarily how it truly is. We imagine that achieving a goal or being with a certain person will feel a certain way, but reality does not always match our expectations.

For example, many people desire fame because it looks glamorous and fulfilling from the outside. But for those who achieve it, fame often feels different, less magical than it seemed. This is because what we desire is often influenced by the way something is projected to us, not by its actual substance. The same is true for personal relationships, career goals, or even material possessions.

Desire, however, is not inherently bad. It can inspire us to grow and achieve incredible things. But it is important to ask ourselves: What do I genuinely want, and why? Are we chasing an illusion, or are we pursuing something that will bring real fulfilment? By reflecting on what lies beneath our desires, we can align them with what truly matters to us, our values, our growth, and our inner peace.

Ambition

Ambition is the drive to achieve something meaningful, often fuelled by a deep desire for growth, success, or recognition. It is what motivates us to set goals and push through challenges. But ambition is complex, it can be both a tool for fulfilment and a trap that keeps us chasing things that do not bring lasting happiness.

True ambition is not about reaching a specific status or milestone; it is about understanding what really matters to us. For example, someone might work tirelessly to climb the career ladder, thinking that a promotion or a certain salary will make them happy. But if the ambition is rooted in external validation, the satisfaction will likely be temporary. The real question is: What part of this goal aligns with my happiness or purpose?

Ambition becomes most powerful when it is tied to authentic joy and fulfilment rather than surface-level rewards. It is not about abandoning ambition it is about being intentional. When we direct our energy toward what genuinely brings us peace and happiness, ambition becomes a source of growth rather than a race we never finish.

Hostility

Hostility is an emotional reaction that most of us have both given and received. It often comes from a place of fear or self-protection, rather than true malice. When someone feels threatened whether by vulnerability, judgment, or past wounds, they might react with anger or defensiveness. It is a shield, a way to keep others out, even if it is not always intentional.

Sometimes, hostility becomes a habit. People who have faced pain or rejection may default to anger because it feels safer than letting someone get too close. But while hostility can be a defence mechanism, it often isolates us further, making it harder to find connection or understanding.

Breaking through hostility requires compassion. When we see someone acting with anger, we can try to ask: What might they be protecting? By approaching others with patience rather than confrontation, we create space for understanding and trust. Hostility does not have to be permanent, it is a wall that can come down when met with kindness and care.

Reclusion

Reclusion is the act of withdrawing from others, often driven by feelings of doubt, fear, or overwhelm. For some, it's a reaction to feeling misunderstood or judged; for others, it might stem from a belief that their presence is a burden. Reclusion can also be a way to protect oneself from vulnerability, creating a safe space where emotions cannot be misinterpreted.

Sometimes, reclusion is temporary a pause to gather strength or reflect. Other times, it becomes a habit, a retreat from the world that feels increasingly hard to leave. It is important to ask: Am I isolating myself because I need time to heal, or because I am afraid to connect?

Reclusion is not inherently negative. When chosen intentionally, it can be a source of peace and clarity. But when it is driven by fear or self-doubt, it can cut us off from the very connection we crave. The key is balance: to allow ourselves moments of solitude while staying open to the warmth and understanding that comes from others. Reclusion, when met with self-compassion and courage, can be a stepping stone toward deeper connection rather than a barrier.

It is also important that we take into consideration peoples attachment/detachment from the conversation we are trying to have, these responses are some of the most vital to observe, as it will allow you to be able to tell if their reactions are genuine or being projected because they are in fact not attached to the intention of the conversation.

We must ensure that we do not allow our intuition to impede or intrude on genuine observation, this is why the true and genuine reading of responses is one of the biggest keys within Touching Souls and Changing Faces. It is also necessary to remove the past ideas of the sense of self you are communicating with, because as we know every person and every environment are constantly adapting and evolving.

It is also worth noting that your own cues and triggers will be being somewhat observed by the self you are communicating with even if only being done subconsciously.

Practice Makes Connection

Understanding the responses we receive is only the first step it is what we choose to do with that understanding that creates real change. Reflection alone can deepen our awareness, but it is through practice that we transform awareness into connection, empathy, and impact. Growth, after all, does not happen just in the mind; it takes root in action.

Practicing connection is not about rigid rules or perfect execution it is about weaving these practices into the unique fabric of your life. These exercises are not a one-size-fits-all solution, and they may take time to feel natural. Some might feel uncomfortable at first, others might reveal unexpected insights, and many will require patience and repetition. But it is in this slow, deliberate integration that transformation begins.

The beauty of practice lies in its imperfections. It is not about getting it "right" every time it is about trying, learning, and improving with each step. Practice is where we build the muscles of empathy and the habits of meaningful impact. Without it, our intentions remain ideas; with it, they become part of who we are.

Take a moment to reflect:

What actions can you take today to bring your reflections to life?

How can you adapt these practices to fit your own rhythm and daily life?

What might change if you approached them with curiosity and patience, rather than urgency?

As you move into the next chapter, consider this.

The exercises ahead are not about perfection but progress. They are tools to help us weave observation and understanding into the fabric of our lives, one deliberate choice at a time. Take your time, adjust them to suit your needs, and remember that connection grows through consistent, thoughtful practice.

Excercises

of Life

The things you can do

Do you often practice your skills you are learning? Have you in the past ever practiced anything like this? Can you observe within yourself right now and say you've ever put in the work to truly aid those you love? I didn't, I learned the hard way. It still isn't easy. But every day it gets a little bit easier.

Let us use these examples below.

The Coffee Shop Observation – Observe the emotional state of the people around you. The people going about their day outside the shop and also the wellbeing in the people on the tables around you. But in my opinion the most beneficial observations are that of the staff, the way they communicate with their colleagues and the way they communicate with customers, notice the nuances of interaction and how they are when not interacting.

The Self Observation - I am here to observe the way my sense of self has been affected today, let us observe.

Out of bubble interactions – Interact with strangers for the benefit of them even if that's just a smile crossing the street. By out of bubble, I simply mean people you would not expect or be expected to communicate with, another way to describe this with an analogy from Chapter 6, it would be out of branch interactions.

The contagious faces – This is a simple experiment the way people describe a smile to be contagious, you will find that so are most emotions when passed directly you can do this in any place however I am sat here practicing this example in a coffee shop as I write this, the confusion face I passed along to the lady at the other end of the café was quickly passed to her server and it was very entertaining. Emotion is powerful so share your brightest.

You would not last a day in my head. – This is a saying I'm sure most of us have either been a victim of giving or receiving. However, when put into perspective we would not be able to last a day in any head other than our own, as we would be completely lost without our coping strategies, structures, and mechanisms for understanding and progressing. For this imagine yourself in the shoes of someone in your surroundings, not to judge but to explore.

The changing of a singular perception. – This is a beautiful exercise of life and that is the positive impact of perception even if only to one person. I went out to do my weekly shopping and divided by our big two meter stickers a little old lady was not aware that she had just cut in front of me as she stood next to and had a good old chat with an apparent friend, when it came to her (my) turn to place the goods on the checkout her friend announced to her that I was waiting and had been behind her for some time. To which I insisted they stay together, and I was more than happy to wait if it allowed them to continue to have a nice time. After buying her goods, she came back as I was about to pay to let the gentleman behind the till know that my actions had restored her faith in the future of Men as she was over time becoming increasingly disappointed with the way men of my generation behave.

This altering of this old ladies perception made my week. It also will have had a leveraged impact on how she communicates to and about the men of my age in the future, impact people, touching souls and changing faces, it is what were here to do.

So do your best to be out of branch and do something that breaks a stereotype, I aim to do this at least once a week.

The Stubborn Sitter. – This is my preferred method of meditation and where the most useful information comes to fruition.

To do this we will be setting a timer, I would recommend thirty minutes, however if you do not have the patience for thirty minutes, I would advise one hour. (My attempt at Abbot humour)

There you will sit and allow your mind to wander and remind yourself you are there to sit and observe every time it does, there you will sit until your self prescribed timer releases you from your internal observations. Hopefully having gained insights, you perhaps would usually try to avoid.

The Circle of Reflection

Every action we take sends energy outward, creating responses that ripple back to us. These responses are not just reactions they are opportunities to reflect, learn, and grow. This exchange, this ongoing cycle of action and reflection, is the rhythm of life. It is how we refine our understanding of ourselves, deepen our connections with others, and navigate the world with greater intention.

Reflection is not the end of a journey; it is the bridge to the next action. When we pause to consider the effects of what we do how it touches others, what it stirs in them, and how they reflect it back to us we gain clarity about our own impact. And that clarity informs the next choice we make, continuing the circle.

This cycle is not linear or perfect. It is fluid and ever-changing, shaped by the unique dynamics of each interaction. At times, our actions may resonate deeply with others, creating a sense of harmony. At other times, the responses may feel challenging, even uncomfortable, offering us valuable lessons about ourselves and the world around us.

Take a moment to reflect:

When you act, do you take time to notice the responses you receive?

How do these responses shape the next action you take?

What would change if you embraced reflection not as a conclusion, but as part of an ongoing, living cycle?

As you move into the next chapter, consider the dynamic interplay of observation, action, and response. Every moment holds the potential to teach us, to shape us, and to bring us closer to the connections we seek. The circle of reflection is always turning; the question is, how will you step into it?

The Book of Rational Thinking

Observations within relationships

Relationships are at the heart of human experience. In this chapter, we will explore two distinct types of relationships:

- Intimate Relationships: These are deep, emotionally significant connections, such as those with romantic partners, close friends, or family members.

- Passive Relationships: These are more casual or fleeting interactions, like those with acquaintances, co-workers, or strangers.

While the primary focus here will be on intimate relationships, the tools of observation apply to both. Now, let us begin by exploring the foundational elements of observing and nurturing these connections.

Prioritising the Self in Intimate Relationships:

In an intimate relationship, making your sense of self a priority is not selfish it is essential. Authenticity forms the foundation of a strong connection. This does not mean the relationship revolves around you, but rather that understanding your own needs and openly communicating them is vital for success.

A thriving relationship requires mutual growth and transparency. Both partners must work toward being their best selves while supporting the other's journey. When you keep your dreams, struggles, or desires to yourself, you risk creating a disconnect. Synchronicity depends on honest communication and a shared commitment to growth.

Reflect for a moment:

Do you feel comfortable sharing your dreams and goals with your partner?

Are you encouraging their growth without neglecting your own?

Stagnation occurs when growth halts either for one partner or the relationship as a whole. Remember, relationships flourish when both individuals continue to evolve together.

Observation is a powerful tool in both intimate and passive relationships. In an intimate relationship, your actions, words, and intentions carry immense weight they can deeply nurture or profoundly hurt your partner.

Ask yourself:

Am I touching their soul and changing their face for the better?

Are my actions fostering connection, or are they unintentionally causing harm?

A useful metaphor is to view your intimate relationship as a well-oiled machine, with intricate moving parts that depend on each other to function. To keep it running smoothly, you must "read the instruction manual" of your partner, their unique needs, fears, and desires. Ignoring this manual can lead to misunderstandings and unintended hurt.

Observation is not just about noticing behaviours; it's about understanding the emotions and intentions behind them.

Love is often seen as an emotion, but it is so much more

than that. Love is an act of pure observation. It is seeing your partner fully, their hopes, flaws, strengths, and vulnerabilities, and reflecting that understanding back to them with care.

At its core, love is also about observing yourself:
What do I see in myself when I am with them?
How does this relationship reveal who I truly am?

Love is the practice of observing with clarity and compassion of self from self, and of "I" from "I."

Here are a few ways to cultivate observation in your relationships:

Daily Check-Ins:

Take a moment each day to ask yourself, how am I showing up in this relationship? and how is my partner feeling today?

Open Conversations: Share your goals and struggles openly with your partner and invite them to do the same.

Mindfulness Practice:

When a moment of conflict arises, pause and observe

before reacting. Ask yourself, what is driving my response? What does my partner need right now?

Every relationship is unique, but the principles of observation, authenticity, and growth are universal. Whether you're navigating an intimate relationship or a fleeting passive interaction, the way you observe and act has the power to Touch Souls and Change Faces for better or worse.

So, the next time you engage with someone, ask yourself:

Am I fostering growth, understanding, and connection? Or am I letting old habits and unspoken assumptions hold us back?

The beauty of relationships, both intimate and passive, lies in the opportunity to learn, grow, and create moments of meaning together. Observation is your greatest tool, use it wisely.

Love is pure observation.

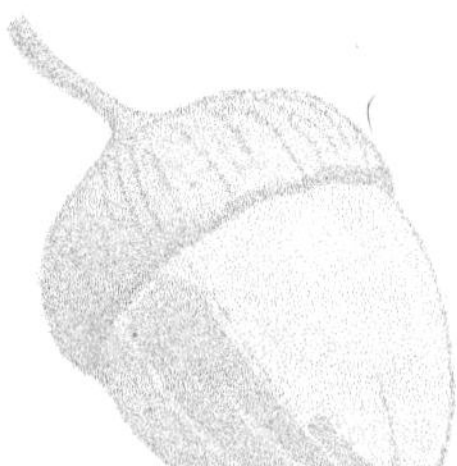

Turning Insight Into Action

Reflection is a powerful tool, but its true value lies in what we do with it. Clarity and understanding are only the beginning, action is where transformation takes root. When we take what we have observed and apply it to our daily lives, we begin to shape the narrative of who we are and who we are becoming.

But what does it mean to take action? Imagine for a moment that your life is a performance. Each choice, each movement, each word is a scene unfolding. Behind every great performance, there are unseen forces at work: direction, intention, and the interplay of elements that create the final result. What guides your decisions? Who or what is crafting the story you live?

The connection between insight and action lies in intention making choices that align with the vision you want to bring to life. The next chapter invites you to explore this balance and begin crafting your story with clarity, creativity, and purpose.

As we step into the next chapter, consider this:

What role are you playing in your own life?

Are you the actor, the director, or something in between?

How do the choices you make today create the story you will look back on tomorrow?

What tools do you have to refine the performance of your own life?

As we explore the practical things you can do in your everyday life in the next chapter it is here we start to untie, detangle and reformat some of the skills we have been exploring and add new dynamics to them in an attempt to bring perspective to not only your sense of self, but your sense of self to others.

A Practical

Use of Skill

The thing you can do now

The Character Exercise:

Now what you are going to do is a practical exercise, what I would like you to do is pick any TV show or movie and put it on, something scripted with characters.

Now observe these characters observe the way what is being said has been scripted by a mind outside of the universe you are observing, see the way what is being said is to provoke the conversation and add longevity to the scene or communication.

Observe the way the actor playing the character is portraying the person in the scene, the way they move with intention and the way they choose to deliver words. The way everything is done with thought and intention, truly see the person playing the character.

Pay attention to what all of the visual cues that have been added by a director may be hinting towards, why they chose to have the camera where it is, the lighting the way it is set and the positioning of the characters.

Look at the way lines have been written and the choice of words used, pay attention to what could be stage direction and what could be actors creative freedom. Do this for 10 - 20 minutes. Observe all of these things fully and bring it all into your awareness, once you have done this for 10 - 20 minutes and only once you have done this for 10 - 20 minutes turn the page.

Now place that idea of person playing a character onto yourself.

Close your eyes and do a stubborn sitter for internal observation, or simply take note of it as you continue to interact through your day.

Stubborn Sitter is highly recommended following this exercise.

Sit yourself down with your timer and the only thing I want you to focus on until your timer runs out is the idea that you are an actor playing the character everyone perceives you to be.

How does that make you feel?

How does the realisation of you being an actor playing your character affect you?

In some religions they believe that this actor is their version of The Almighty, The Observer, the sense of (I) and the 'Self' the you that is everything you entail your Past, your trauma every connotation that comes with your entity is the character your (I) is playing.

The Art of Truly Seeing

Observation begins with noticing, but to truly see is an act of depth and presence. Seeing is more than just recognizing what is in front of us it is understanding what lies beneath, the layers of meaning and intention that shape what we perceive. It is an art, a skill that grows sharper the more we practice it, and a lens through which we can better know both the world and ourselves.

True seeing requires stillness and courage. It challenges us to see others as they are, not as we expect them to be, and to look inward with the same honesty. To truly see is to embrace nuance, to sit with what is uncomfortable, and to find beauty in what is overlooked.

Reflect for a moment:

When was the last time you felt truly seen by someone else? What made it meaningful?

How often do you take the time to look beyond the surface in your daily life?

What might change if you chose to see yourself, others, and the world with deeper intention?

As we now progress towards the end of our book, the final straight if you will remember how individual and unique this journey is, you are, and the others you come into contact with. All leaves beautifully vibrant in their different shades, all changing with the seasons but all a contributor to our beautiful whole, humanity.

The Observation of Seeing

The skills of submitting to I

The I removes the (me) I, leaving just the authentic I. Only the I referring to consciousness (witnessing) is the true I.

Now this came from one of Mooji's Saatsangs teachings. Mooji is someone I highly recommend you spend some time observing as his insights have been of great help to both myself and the people I know along their journey to understanding.

"The ghost of self is bothering me,
The ghost is bothering you or you are bothered by the ghost?"

Think about that for a moment your mind attacks may be trying to teach you something and it could be a case of you are bothered by them rather than they are bothering you.

**"Nothing you are conscious of can be the I.
The mind that is bothered by the ghost mind is also an illusion."**

This provoked an analogy within me that I hope will allow you to have a further understanding. "The Hands Of Perspective."

Hold up an open hand in front of your face (A) this will represent your character. Now take your other hand (B) and place it between your character hand and your face (C), we will now turn this middle hand (B) into a mouth, truly see the open hand as the self (character) and your eye as the observer, now imagine the self hand being willed through coping mechanisms and emotional responses and now use the hand in the middle to communicate the way this makes your observer feel.

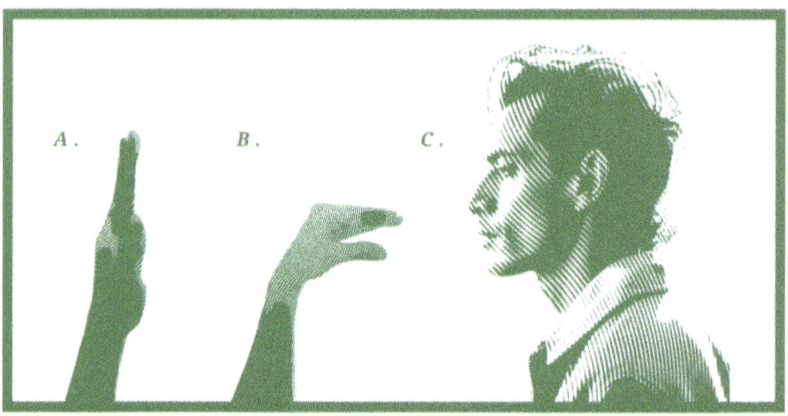

Now accept that the observing communicator hand in the middle is another projection of self that is and has been affected by observing, the real observer (I) is not and cannot be affected or influenced.

This middle perspective as we are going to call it is the General and it will instruct and influence your character in day-to-day life, we now need to get to a point where we can observe this and see where it is for the betterment or detriment of self. The important thing to understand is that the middle perspective is not your sense of I, it is not your observer. It is another projection or manifestation of your sense of self. While It is incredible that you can notice this and it will play a huge part in your understanding of yourself and will ultimately make your everyday interactions and communications a lot easier with a rounded level of observation and understanding, we are going to delve into finding our comfort and happiness within our sense of simply I, our I Am.

Finding our middle observer, it is important to point out that this is our product of conditioning, the way we communicate to ourselves on a daily basis and have been doing our entire lives, the conditioning of how things make us feel and what is supposed to be our reactions to triggers, it is just as important to understand this as it is to understand that your character is a product of environment and circumstance. Our character and our middle perspective are both products of circumstances that were predominantly not done to ourselves by ourselves. In order to find peace within this, the key is to realise that finding your sense of I is not a removal of self, it is simply a pure observation of self.

Find the stillness in the unprovoking observation, and peace will be found within yourself.

Authenticity – don't be a representative of self, be your true self (I).

Aren't all these characters, including your own, including the character that is affected by your observations a beautiful thing to observe.

Remember in chapter two where we observed with a removal of our sense of self? It is difficult but very important and truly magical.

Back to The Hands of Perspective.

- I (you looking at your hands.)
- Flat Hand (Self Character, Your person for people.)
- Talking Hand (you communicating to I about Self)

If all this hand does is nag, and degrade, that's self-destructive, this hand is your biggest fan and greatest enemy dependent on how you dictate your perception of character to your sense of I. It is but a mirror of inward communication and perception.

Shifting Perspectives

Seeing is shaped by where we stand. Our viewpoint influences everything, what we notice, what we value, and what we overlook. But what happens when the tables turn, and we are invited to step into another perspective? These moments, though often uncomfortable, are the ones that shape us most deeply.

Perspective shifts ask us to question the truths we hold tightly and to embrace ambiguity. To see the world through another's eyes is to challenge the limits of our empathy and broaden the scope of our understanding.

Reflect for a moment:

When has someone challenged you to see something differently? How did it feel?

What perspectives in your life might you be avoiding, and why?

How can stepping into another's viewpoint teach you something about your own?

Moving on into 'The book of turned tables' the final entry into section three, pause for a moment. Thing about the journey you have been on,

and where you would want your personal journey to lead. This life we live is our story, it is our moment to moment highlight reel of existence. Every day a chance to awake fresh, every interaction an opportunity to impact someone for the better, and every challenge a moment that could become a catalyst for growth.

The Book of Turned Tables

What will be will be

There are as many paths to understanding as there are people seeking it. Trust your process, your journey, and the unique way it unfolds for you. Your path is correct for you, even when it feels unclear or challenging. Begin by noticing when you are playing an expected character. Pay attention to how it feels to be aware of that role and to step outside it, even briefly and observe the ways it serves or limits you.

What Will Be, Will Be

We often fight against reality, believing that if we resist or struggle hard enough, we can reshape it. But true freedom lies in surrendering to the flow of life, not inaction but intentional action rooted in trust rather than fear or expectation. Acceptance does not mean passivity, it is an act of profound strength to let go of control and align yourself with the rhythm of life.

When you allow yourself to trust what will be, you create the space to act authentically. Resistance clouds the path; surrender clears it.

Playing the Expected Character

We all wear masks, consciously or unconsciously. These personas the caregiver, the achiever, the pleaser, all serve a purpose, but they can also confine us. They become roles we default to, especially in moments of uncertainty, often at the expense of our truest selves.

Ask yourself:
What role do I feel I am playing right now?

How does this role serve me?
How does it hold me back?

Awareness is the key to stepping out of autopilot. When you notice the character you are playing, you create the opportunity to choose authenticity instead. Authenticity is not about rejecting the roles we play; it is about understanding them and deciding when to step beyond them.

The answers are already within you.

What you are searching for is not something to be found outside yourself. It has always been there, waiting to be uncovered. Imagine your true self as a treasure buried beneath layers of sand, layers formed by societal expectations, fear of judgment, or unresolved pain. Your journey is not about creating something new but gently removing what obscures the treasure.

This process is not always easy. Sometimes it feels monotonous, sometimes frustrating, but these moments are part of the unearthing. In monotony, you find patience. in frustration, you stumble upon resilience. Each grain of sand removed reveals more of your true self.

Reflect:

What blinds you to your true self?

What small step can you take today to clear even one layer?

Comfortability in the familiarity of uncomfortability.

It is paradoxical, but humans often find comfort in familiar discomfort. Whether it is a toxic relationship, a self-limiting belief, or a habitual reaction, we cling to what we know, even when it harms us. The unknown feels riskier than the pain we have learned to endure.

Take a moment to consider:
What discomfort in your life feels strangely familiar?
What would stepping out of that pattern look like, even for a moment?

Breaking free does not require drastic change. Start small challenge one familiar discomfort today. Say no where you usually say yes.

Pause before reacting in a way that feels automatic. These moments of intentional change create the conditions for growth.

Practical Reflections and Exercises

Daily Awareness Practice: At the end of each day, reflect on where you acted authentically and where you defaulted to a role. Write down what you notice.

Journaling Prompt: Think of a time when you were most aware of playing a character. How did it feel? What might have changed if you acted differently?

Mindfulness Exercise: When frustration or monotony arises, pause. Do not resist it; sit with it. Ask yourself: What does this feeling reveal about me?

Your journey is your own, and you are exactly where you need to be. Progress is not linear, and transformation is not immediate. The next time you find yourself playing an expected character, pause. Ask: Who am I beneath this role? What would it feel like to act as my truest self right now?

Trust the path beneath your feet, even when it feels uncertain. Every step, every pause, every moment of clarity or confusion is bringing you closer to the essence of who you are. What will be, will be, and within that truth lies the freedom to grow.

Finding Peace in Progress

Progress is not always something we measure in actions or achievements; sometimes, it is found in moments of quiet reflection. The words we carry with us the ones we return to for comfort, for clarity, for inspiration can become the anchors that guide us through life's currents.

This next chapter is a collection of those words, a space to pause and breathe. Each stanza, each poem, reflects stillness and motion, of growth and grounding.

Reflect for a moment:

What words or thoughts have brought you peace in moments of uncertainty?

When was the last time you paused to let stillness shape your understanding?

How can you create space for reflection in the busyness of your everyday life?

When reading through words of tranquil progress, take them at your own pace, digest them, dissect them, analyse what they mean to you. They all came from a moment, were all provoked by an emotion. They are my outpouring from I to self, and sometimes a cry from self to I.

Words of Tranquil Progress

From I to Self.

When preparation meets opportunity, success is inevitable.

We are individually and collectively the consciousness that makes up our simulation.

You are the greatest teacher, for you are responsible for everything you will ever know.

If you are not being authentic, silence the voices, for it is not time to project yourself.

Live in the now and you will be everfresh in every moment.

Even the best intentions at heart can be counterproductive when contradicting the intention of the self you are aiding. Any time conflict is reciprocated, it can only prohibit progress.

Set your table, take with you the utensils needed for the meal, do not just wait at tables, never be the waiter of all tables.

The problems arose when memory became the leader of progress, project forwards.

Within this world, do not be a senseless I, senseless eyes will not touch souls and change faces for the better.

Provoke healing within the world, before the world provokes death within you.

Touch Souls & Change faces, for the betterment of all, including oneself.

This life is more than the sum of what your I is witness to of the global sitcom.

Every action once interpreted foreshadows its ending. You are more than the I that perceives itself, we, are the I that perceives.

Take the butterfly effect, make this moment your past future, make those small impacts that shape your new future.

My Soul is a Jigsaw I will continue to learn to love the pieces.

You are not broken,
Friction warms your clay,
You do not need fixing,
You need time to mould.

Everyone you have ever admired,
Moulded themselves from the same clay as you.

Do not get lost in the impact that happens to you,
There is so much life to happen constantly.
You are more than everything you have been through,

Your worth is more than the sum you can accumulate, It is what you can give from what you have been through.
You never have to survive another of your darkest days.
Bonus, from them you have already learned.

I have no need to dwell on situations that can be concluded as inconclusive.

He who vanquishes the spider,
Is destined to suffer the fly.

Unless willing to fall as an acorn again,
The mighty oak is destined for lumbar.

We are at the Mercy of the breeze, we can curve to choose which way we are blown, we are the leaf.

Time, Distance, Good & Evil are constructs invented for the concept of human regulation.

They gave me shape and form,
When I arrived, I was simply now,
This is why to them,
The devil is in the details
For alone I am viewed as comparable to other,
Though the whole, I am.

Do not go walking through life trying to grab every piece.
Just keep aiming, stepping and watch,
It might be supposed to fall in behind you.

As a parent you should raise your children to be better than you. Seek inspiration in their innovation. It does not matter if you are 30, 50 or 80, you do not finish learning to be a better human being.

Your reservations can be viewed as passivity by those who do not think in the language of impact.

As you peer through the dew glistened web of life,
The sun articulates the universe in every reflection and refraction.

It comes in waves
It is guided like the way that waves guard a tide,
It is mighty.
It leaves or stays,
It comes in waves,
Speaking heart and knowledge,
Learn what it says,
Its time never truly expires,
Even if memory fades,
Its mystical power never leaves us,
It is more powerful than between us,
It comes in waves,
Its order is tall,
It can be your power,
You shine on all

Staying Grounded in the Journey

As we explore ideas and reflections, it is easy to become consumed by the depth of what we uncover. But reflection is not meant to overwhelm; it is meant to illuminate.

Reflect for a moment:

Have you allowed yourself space to pause and reflect without judgment?

How can you stay connected to the grounding forces in your life, even as you explore deeper questions?

This next chapter takes a step back, a moment to breathe and to remind yourself that no single book, idea, or reflection has all the answers. Growth is not about perfection, and understanding does not come all at once. To remain grounded is to hold these truths lightly, allowing them to guide you without letting them consume you.

That which Could have been Lost

Lost in communication

Hello, From a different time, it has been a few years now since my initial completion of Touching Souls & Changing faces, Time spent living with its practices in writing and an ongoing effort to share the love and ethos with others, and what a time it has indeed been. The years have helped me reframe, rephrase and rework the book into what I now proudly present you with.

The serpents kiss came in many forms, though the years were constant, I made it through one hundred percent of the hardest days, not a single tear fallen was wasted, not a single emotion was rejected and not learned from, although at times they may have been avoided, this in itself was a lesson, take it as it comes not when you feel like getting round to it.

The constant will Is movement. I have often heard people say in a huge universe full of galaxies I'm a speck of dust on a floating rock.

In this ever-expanding universe of atoms consciously doing their job, we are the only collection of atoms we know of capable of perceiving and interpreting itself as a collection.

Think about the billions of atoms that make up you, all consciously bound in place, making you able to be the self you use to interpret.

What we are is beautiful, what we are is rare, what we are is a statistical impossibility, keep breaking statistics, keep achieving the impossible.

Remember its Billions to 1 of this moment existing, so even if you only see the tiniest opportunity, you have more of a chance of creating that than the chance of you existing. you are the collective power.

"You did not come into this world; you came out of it."
-Alan Watts

"Everything will always collectively code our reality."
-Samuel Witty

The Journey Is Yours

Every step you have taken through these pages has been uniquely your own. No two journeys are the same, even when they tread similar paths. The reflections you have embraced, the questions you have pondered, and the insights you have gained are yours to carry forward in a way that feels right for you.

This journey has not been about providing definitive answers but offering perspectives and tools to help you see yourself and others with more clarity, more empathy, and more intention. What you do with those tools now is entirely up to you.

Reflect for a moment:

What ideas or moments from this book have resonated most deeply with you?

How have your perceptions shifted since you began this journey?

What will you carry forward into the next chapter of your life?

The end of this book is not the end of the journey; it is a pause, a moment to gather yourself before stepping back into the world. The tools, reflections, and connections you have found here are just beginnings. What happens next is a story only you can write.

Conclusion

Within you, yes YOU, there is a divinity, and you are powerful. You matter and ultimately you are all that matters. Maintain your happiness however possible and go forth on a new adventure, an adventure of the ever-fresh world and continue the purpose,

Touch Souls and Change Faces.

One final piece of advice would be this.

View each morning as a beautiful flower bud, be at peace as you continue to watch it bloom from there.

Now, we have discussed our observations, we have learned our skills and the practical use of them, we can read and relate to our loved ones and live with our best interests at heart. We can live with our intention of touching souls & Changing Faces, we can view our relationships as well-oiled machines, and we can see this is also our relationships with ourselves.

We understand that in us we have love, lust, trauma, desire and many things we use to cope and deal with life, but we also understand and see them for what they are.

We can use these tools to aid others to see every day as everfresh and inspire them to watch the world bloom around them.

We understand at the simplest level that our lives have purpose.

I will not pretend your road will be easy, and I will not pretend mine is either. I will not lie to you it is ever changing, but everfresh. I still do not fully understand, and I do not expect you to either, but this exploration of life, self and I, along with impact and resonance is all we really have.

With love, from

SAMWELL

Epilogue.
where he still finds me.

I used to think the divine was something you had to chase, a light somewhere far off that only the pure could reach. But life, in its mercy, keeps proving otherwise.

God doesn't hide in heaven. He hides in the small things.
In my son's laughter. In the quiet between words.
In the way pain softens once you've let it teach you.

This book was once my cry for help. Now it's my thank you.

For every page I thought would be my last, He turned into another reason to stay.
For every question I wrote, He answered with breath, with presence, with you still reading.

And though I could have rewritten it all, reshaped it with new understanding. I chose not to. Because these words were born of a moment that needed no polish.
They were written by hands that were shaking, but sincere.

Maybe that's enough.
Maybe it's not about perfect words or tidy endings.
Maybe it's just about being willing to speak, and to keep living long enough to listen back.

www.samwellworldwide.com

Touching Souls and changing faces

www.ingramcontent.com/pod-product-compliance
Ingram Content Group UK Ltd.
Pitfield, Milton Keynes, MK11 3LW, UK
UKHW020115020326
468525UK00003B/49

9 781919 333304